HOW FESTIVE THE AMBULANCE

HOW FESTIVE THE AMBULANCE

KIM FU

NIGHTWOOD EDITIONS

2016

Nightwood Editions
P.O. Box 1779
Gibsons, BC VON 1VO
Canada
www.nightwoodeditions.com

COVER DESIGN & TYPOGRAPHY: Carleton Wilson

Nightwood Editions acknowledges financial support from
the Government of Canada through the Canada Book Fund and
the Canada Council for the Arts, and from the Province of British Columbia
through the British Columbia Arts Council and the Book Publisher's Tax Credit.

This book has been produced on 100% post-consumer recycled,
ancient-forest-free paper, processed chlorine-free
and printed with vegetable-based dyes.

Printed and bound in Canada.

CIP data available from Library and Archives Canada.

ISBN 978-0-88971-321-5 · 0-88971-321-9

FOR THE FU WOMEN:
MY MOTHER, SISTERS AND NIECES

CONTENTS

SMALL CRIMES OF A NORTHERN PEOPLE

WHY THIS PLACE AND NOT ANOTHER

CREATURES GREAT & SMALL

I have a forgettable face. It allows me to belch in public, to fart, to wipe snot on my sleeve, because I don't know these people and they won't remember me. I order meatball subs with marinara sauce and racks of ribs and uncracked lobsters, any food that might merit a bib, because no one is watching. I slurp anything that can be slurped. I hold up the grocery line counting out my pennies, which—even though she just listened to me run through my eleventy-twelves and sickity-nons— the cashier has to count again. I stretch across three seats on the bus and whack the lap of a man in a wheelchair, looking for the snooze button. I introduce myself four times before you remember. What luxury to be not tall not short not fat not thin, above all not beautiful, to have the same face as Charlie Brown: dot, dot, quivering line of anguish. I get to be disgusting. What does the little red-headed girl get? She's counting her valentines, talking in a grown-up's *wah-wah* voice. She's always off-camera, where perfection lives.

I imagined them in small, idle rooms, sharpening their beaks with nail files, women that *love too much*, as on a magazine cover: women, do you love too much? On the desks and patterned-papered walls, rotary phones that don't ring and require a switchboard. Doors with knockers glued in place and disconnected doorbells. I imagined them waiting for me in a universe where there are no other activities, or all other activities are meaningless, and every action is inverted into denial: don't eat for me, ladies, wring the oil from your feathers, ladies, don't sing for me, ladies, save your voice. My life, meanwhile, like a boar in a china shop. Behold the fragile things that shatter on my tusks and bucking hooves! Worship the god of destruction! Then they descended. Instead of nipping at the ticks on my back, grooming my bristles and dropping fattened worms into my mouth, instead of riding my back wherever I felt like going, they lifted me in their talons like predatory eagles, like I was a mere fish who could suffocate by the gills. They were silent, swift, black. Their mothers stayed on the telephone wire, watched the spectacle. A murder of mothers with that look in their eyes: *You should have known, pig. You should have known.*

I.

Sad-face clowns play accordion, euphonium and clarinet,
joyless Balkan melodies in a minor key. Audience volunteers
are tricked into digging a pit at centre ring.
The lions are losing their hair, dry cough
instead of roar. Wolf children sniff along the ground,
eat discarded popcorn kernels and snarl convincingly
until a lady in the front row shrieks, *These are real children!*
I am the star attraction, the pig-man,
bristle-bearded, faintly familiar: were we once neighbours?
Did you leave your daughters with me during an emergency—
your wife had heart palpitations and you didn't know
if it was serious, and you had seen me,
reading on my porch, sweeping leaves, quiet, knowable,
well-intentioned in the way of the elderly—
PIG MAN! you scream, as loud as you know how.

II.

The children were always wolves, fairy-tale tricksters,
bursting out of cloaks with bits of grandma in their teeth,
huffing and puffing while I watched through the windows
of my solid brick house. They used to believe my stories.
I sent them to the pristine beaches of my childhood
(the water now choked with red algae, primordial soup
sucking them under, higher mammals with tumours
where their eyes should be, slick tributaries on fire),
sold them useless toys, convinced them that
boredom was sickness and I had the cure.
Now they stalk through the streets in ski masks,
furry snouts protruding from cut holes,
smashing storefronts and calling for me.
PIG MAN! they cry, voices cracking pubescent:
You will pay for what you've done.
My house holds fast. I get old and older. They forget
you cannot extort the dead. The belly is bacon,
the organs are sweetbreads. The mind is the brain
and the brain is for aspic.

plays pretend at the bridal shop.
They pull the gowns on carefully
so her horn doesn't pierce the tulle,
so the cupcake bustle and spreading trains
drape across her back half and all four legs.
She nickers in pleasure at her reflection,
tells the long story of how she met
her imaginary fiancé, describes the venue
in quotes from a magazine:
weathered wood demands muslin drapes,
centrepieces alternate roses and curly willow.

She goes to open houses to riffle through drawers,
to pocket tchotchkes and sniff the sheets.
She divines meaning from the way the chairs face
toward or away from the southern light.
She knows these people, as she knows the ones
on the Home & Garden channel:
sledgehammering through walls and revealing
their sodden, infested, but fixable souls.

She dyes her mane with Kool-Aid, and the pink runs.
She applies gold spray paint to her horn each morning,
hoping to imitate the brass tusks
on the unicorns skewered to the carousel,
their brittle, painted smiles, harnesses
embedded in their backs and shellacked to high gloss.
Her horn still has the unsettling texture of a tooth,
the suggestion of a living core, a warm and pulsing root.

1. Infancy as a human

I've seen this waist-high grass
and weeping tree before, in a drugstore frame
and a Bollywood movie, the trunk a pivot point
for coquettish hide-and-seek. On the cover
of *Vanity Fair* it had a swing,
just two ropes and a plank, a girl levitating
on the tip of her coccyx. Poofy virginal
white dress, elegant lipstick slash, Cubist chin,
she had it all. Someone proposed here,
votive candles in a heart, a flowered trellis;
it went viral on the internet and spawned
a thousand thousand proposals. Someone
has decided this is a place where no one
can be ugly, this lonely hillside that bears
but one tree, one strand of sweetgrass,
summer sun fixed at one low angle,
stuck like broken spotlight. The branches
ache to be free of their heavy greenery,
to winter for once. Shorn, fallen and bare.

11. A wedding

The gatekeeper for the mole people
peers at me over his pink nose, an intimate
bulb of mucus membrane, a mane of whiskers:
perceptive and multidirectional. I cite
my poor vision, hold my hands
in dirt-scoop formation, show off my nails,
grown long and hard and yellow
as curls of cold butter. *A delicate
affectation*, he says, but he steps aside.
The towers of their metropolis rise like
a dirt-castle sand castle, musty warm
from the inflamed earth. The black forest
of a black forest cake, spongy peat
that bounces back. They cannot look at each other.
Courtship is a blind forward groping.
The mole prince runs his translucent claws
down the useless heavy dimpled doughy
flesh of my backside, finds stubby legs
coated in velvet fur: we are in love. He tenderly
gouges out my eyes.

III. An empty nest

We rise from the burrow in spring,
me and my pups, old for mole children,
one month weaned and eager to tunnel
out on their own, a world of infinite depth
and possibility. In their bravado,
they forget oxygen; they'll learn.
My prince makes his high-pitched yelps
elsewhere, flushing females out
from the solitary forgetting that makes up
the bulk of our days. Will I recognize the tree
by its roots? That terrible nexus
of too many kinds of beauty. Like Bugs Bunny,
I keep failing to make a left,
churning the Albuquerque sand
like a delusional gardener. I'm sure
the desert is pretty in its way.

iv. A retirement home

I meet a mermaid. We commiserate,
half-rodent to half-fish, as she hugs the shoreline
and I hover at the topsoil, border between
above ground and below. She says the rebellion
has come, describes the scene for the benefit
of my scooped-out darkness. The mole people
walk upright, she says, a spreading pestilence
that overturns crops and claims the upper kingdoms
as their own. The merfolk flop up on beaches,
undulate on unseen waves, raise tridents for war.
They won't accept another treaty:
You may walk among us if you walk on swords,
if your feet bleed, and you dissolve to foam
when we tire of watching you dance.
I twitch my nose to and fro. I smell nothing.
Can't an old mermatron dream? she laughs.
She strokes my downy back. She concedes,
no, we are staying in our place, as ever always.

STAGEHANDS

I.

He'll be a real Canadian yet.
In this toddler's garden of innocuous nouns
emotions are drawn in just mouths and eyes.
Tense confusion
makes him seem innocent.
Unable to tell the difference
between *What did you do last winter?*
and *What do you do in winter?*
he does not reply,
I buried my wife.
He smiles,
thinking it is a general question,
a test of cultural knowledge.
And he knows this one.
What does one do in winter
here, where winter is a thing.
One skis, skates, snowshoes.

II.

At night, he rips off his Velcro eyebrows,
undoes the straps of his silicone belly,
and hangs it on the wall. The body hair
rubs off with a hard sponge. He gargles,
spits, and his accent—too thick
not to question its veracity, really—
sticks like phlegm to the edge of the drain.
Russia is not a real country. Then
he goes to the Club
for Beautiful Men.
Stagehands add one more layer
of orange cooking grease to the wall
behind the stove, take a fine chisel
to the filaments of the aquamarine
1970s fridge. The illusion
of slow appliance death.
They paint mustard stains
on his white undershirt, then rub them in
deeper, as though someone once
tried to wash them out.

We sit in the Joker's dressing room, taking hits off a canister of Joker Venom. He says, "The best love stories are unconsummated. That's why Romeo and Juliet sucked." He giggles, today somewhere between Mark Hamill and Tigger from *Winnie the Pooh*: "Hoo hoo hoo!" The PA lies dead in the corner: scooped-out sickle face, upper gums and all his teeth on display, eyes rolled back in a forever paroxysm of glee. We've built up an immunity. We will never be that happy.

Joker's many tongues writhe living on a rack. One long and pointed, devil-dagger. One too wide for his mouth, making him slurp and lisp. Many tongues of ordinary men, where he lurks most often.

Streetlamp shadows gone to morning. I am short again and eighty years old. "You don't look a day over thirty-five," he coos. Death as consummation. "I can kill everyone you love," he says. "They're all so boring. I can do this—" He lifts my mask to kiss me on the nose. This mask shows only my exquisite jawline. He bites, gently, rests the guillotine pressure of his teeth. I glance at the vanity mirror as he pulls away, expecting a lipstick mark that isn't there. Sweat cuts a canyon down his temple. This Joker wears white powder, but his lips are permanently candy apple red. By accident, nature or design.

"Why don't we ever do this in *your* room?" He knows why: the wall of Robins, the rebuke of their well-adjusted all-American faces and healthy grief. Else their graves and madness, else their abandonment, too much failure for daylight.

He pouts. "You're no fun lately." He offers the gift basket the PA brought: muffins and jam. A butter knife with a jaunty plaid ribbon tied round the handle. "I know. Let's pretend we're virgins again. Let's pretend it's our first time." I take the knife. I ram the dull blade into one of the hollow spots in his torso, avoiding the organs. I stop just a few inches in. Hold with ninja stillness. He moans. "Such control, Bats, *dar*ling. Such control."

A DOG, TETHERED TO A FENCE

bobs, bows a prostrate prayer,
leaps toward a smell. He tests the railing
and the body configurations it allows.
Joy writhes like worms beneath his skin,
relaxes his jowls, rounds his eyes,
perks his tail like a flagpole.
Another dog approaches and he loses his mind.
Near and wildly desired, no contact. Then gone
and forgotten, back to the two-foot diameter
circle of leash. His ears,
exposed, receptive pink canals,
swivel and search like satellite dishes,
and the signals come in strong:
too much, too wonderful!
He digs at the concrete,
he wears the pads of his paws raw.

He has skunk markings on his back
and the blue eyes of a demon.
He unravels miles of rope from my collar,
enough to circumnavigate the earth, and says,
I give you the world. He howls, dances.
I stay paralyzed by the fence post, waiting to go home.

CRADLE SONGS

There are a finite number of places. Of cities, kitchens, holes in mud. Names in the atlas, conquered veldts and travelled rivers. There must be a place where your anus doesn't bleed from a disease of excess or need. We may call them both suffering; it's alright. There is a place where your ideal self walks barefoot, gleams like a colt. Where there is no need to cap your head like a yellowing tooth, to trim your talons and wings. Where we eat more than nothing and less than oil. Where there are no treadmills or severed toes. Where we are fed to birds without formaldehyde. Where there is sleep.

How festive the ambulance looks
studded with jewel-coloured lights,

ruby and amber on the outer rim of a Ferris wheel.
Carnival riders tilted up to the fireworks: *Whee! Ooh. Whee! Ooh.*

What a reassuring shape
like an arctic bear gone vague in the fog,

wide, rounded shoulders in spirit white.

My father's hair was black a year ago.

Not "salt and pepper" but—at most—fresh powder on asphalt,
foam on a midnight sea. Black ground, white stars.

A year ago my father was the bear,
the graceless, lumbering swimmer in the ice floes

who surfaces nose-first, trailing steam.
Now the hair is faint as lanugo on a newborn seal,

now the wasted fields sprout ash blond,
now paralyzed by nerve damage, his eyes roll

as though every word is a sarcastic aside.
The bear stumbles to a cliff edge,

falls without drama or intention—that's life—

outcropping branches and rocks tear away fur,
leave blank patches of flesh. The bear shrinks.

At the bottom, his small, battered remains
rise to walk. The sirens sing

their sweet confirmation: *not-dead, not-dead, not-dead.*

DEAR RACHEL, I BORROWED YOUR CAR

Dear Rachel,
I'm sorry.
We took her out back,
sang her some songs,
put her in neutral
and watched her roll off the pier.

First ecstasy between roommates and neighbours.
Foreign radio through walls, too loud to be exotic,
all in need: shouts of who owes who, for what.
Vocal infection on the airshaft. Stark overcast light,
spilling like seed. Her long hair catches in your mouth,
dry, a grove of mangos: resinous and sweet.
Where did you learn those phrases?
Unbuckling their armour of abstraction
as she peels away a white T-shirt. Underneath,
lean, straightforward bodies of truth.
Love, you choke. Later, an interrogation light,
and the opportunity to recant. Perhaps in court,
perhaps to friends craving coherent narrative,
perhaps before God. Playing a tape recording:
young breathless garbled voices. You lean in,
only able to make out *yes* and *yes* and *yes* again.

HOMETOWN

Flatland cracks scorched in by sun:
if there was ever oil, there isn't now.
Dust clouds thicker than lamplight,
caved mines of ordinary rock.
It's her job to comb out the tumbleweed,
empty troughs of rainwater,
mix mortar for crumbling chimneys,
sweep the dovecote of skeletons.
The postman doesn't ride out this far,
his horse wouldn't make it.
Some lesser creature without eyes,
rib cage cleaved into reaching claws:
she removes it from the road.
Crop sagging, a flat-throated vulture
stays close, awaiting the last holdout.
Each day, in the saloon,
she rolls the piano against the wall,
stacks tables, polishes unused glass.
Flicks the red light on then off,
remembering lurid cheekbones,
rivers of whiskey, sweeping crinoline.
Heeled boots exiting in ragtime.

SALT

At eighteen, they ripened,
lush hips spreading outward, thighs a deep green,
thick with juices, to be tasted, bruised.
Preparing, ancestrally, to squat and bear down
fruit.

But she is pissing on a stick in a mall bathroom stall
wishing her body were filled with sand
and not this humid, fertile darkness:
the black soil of equatorial Amazon.
The craving
for life.

She goes. On an anonymous bus
out toward the wasteland.
There is not another soul
for miles. Not even the father of a ghost.
Skulls smaller than her palm
and the cracked bones of shapeless girls
lie bleached white in the sun.
They salt the earth
while she looks away. And then
out the clinic doors
into the hard desert light.

BEAUTY

The walls of this café are opium-den red,
richer than the wine. The waitress,
half-Ukrainian and half-Parisian,
wears lace with a high, pointed elegance,
the sharp lift of her nose, her breasts.
She must ride a slim ten-speed through the rain,
lean it against the back door,
shake her hair dry and tie a white apron over her hips
as the boy smoothing crepe batter with a straight edge
blushes and burns.
We raise our glasses: chunks of sangria-soaked apple still crisp,
and everyone is smiling, in the peculiar brand of darkness
cut by one candle reflected on glossy wood.
Our empty plates
sit in satisfied shadow.
Everything shines without regret.

LANDING GEAR

It's impossible for a plane to land softly,
for wheels to kiss the ground
shy as a grace note, a sinking embrace.
To change from vertical to lateral
in a perfectly smooth curve

without a lurch, a bashing hello,
a sudden awareness of speed: how fast
you flew through controlled airspace,

yet it seemed like drifting.
Quilt patches of farmland and
hair-seam mountain ranges passed
languidly as strolling cats.
Too high for *high*, more like *elsewhere*,
another dimension, subject
to its own secretive forces, notions of time.

Then you roar across
the uncurved surface at familiar scale,
all its clutter and potential for disaster.

There is sky, earth,
and nothing between.
A border of zero thickness.
On-off. Stepwise. You cannot
transition gently, in peace.

The dead don't look asleep.
They don't fall and stay asleep.
I don't know how that fiction began.

Like a two-language bible, like annotated Shakespeare: these double columns of text. Stir-fried beef and rice noodle/*Gong-chow-noi-hai*. Titles of psalms. In the future, who will know what one side says? Only pictographs and reconstructions. This menu a Rosetta Stone for our lost arbitrary system, our variable hooks and serifs and curlicues more complex than the Mayans'. Stinky Tofu in Joyful Sauce loses its irony when babies choose from a list of acceptable names. In the classrooms of tomorrow, starved youth will be asked to imagine a culture that kept thin pamphlets of poetry pinned to a metal box full of food, who honoured their gods of plenty by describing ingredients in lush language, recounting which chickens ran free, which ones ate flax, which ones lived and died in the dark.

When it gets too hot, the body produces the illusion of cold. Too cold, the illusion of heat. Capillaries open and choose what warrants blood and what can be shed, all while sending the message that you are burning, your clothes are branding irons: strip down and be free. Too much pain, and the illusion of mercy, an opiate crossfire. Too much hunger, and the belly aches with swelling, air and internal fluids take on the weight of food, overfull to bursting.

Imagine the dreams of the whale as it fell to the bottom. Not the bottom slipping out from under you as you got shorter and shorter on a childhood beach. Not the bottom they saw from submarine windows as bolts caved to the pressure, and they drank deep of what they thought was oxygen. The true bottom, where nothing has ever needed sight, and the heat of the earth's core is as near as mirage fire to a man lying frozen and naked in the snow. Down where these eyeless aliens will have the greatest meal of their lives, consume the whale more fully than any human culture ever could, make new the idea of *using every part*. Eat past the bone, inside the bone, inside the dust of existence. Tear away fleshy strips, white clouds of protein, down to the illusion of sunlight, song and baleen plates full of thick-bodied fish.

Backlit panorama of blue sky and treetops
on the ceiling above the MRI machine.
La traviata comes through faintly,
headphones wrapped in woven tissue paper,
the same sanitized fabric as the gown and pillowcase.
The tenor sings *libiamo, libiamo!*
Let us drink! Let us drink!
A shadow voice to the skull-rattling *kachunk-thunk*,
the DO NOT STARE INTO THE LASER sticky label
two inches from the eye. Sung from a booming belly
yet uncertain, elevator Muzak played soft
and low as a hallucination.

I think of you, who died.
That comes first, with its own operatic rhythm,
easy to rhyme: you died. You did other things,
you lay patiently inside many machines,
resisted staring into the laser, shivered thin.
You drew their innards, builder and designer,
as they later drew yours, exposed your faulty wiring,
your speckled organs and blackened brain.
You did other things, but then you died.

Grief rises from the unstirred deep,
not as it used to, not like a man-shaped monster
dripping with bog weeds. As a vision:
I am the technician behind the glass,
you are alone as you will always be alone.

I turn up the music. I have that power,
to make it swell in the chorus:
In questo paradiso ne scopra
il nuovo di.
Let the new day find us
in this paradise.

I can make the sky spread over the tiles,
fluff the picture-frozen clouds
until they travel on the wind.
I can make the thin fluorescent filaments
into a near and beloved star.
I can make the treetops rustle, send flocks
of bird silhouettes across the burning blue.
I am a limited god. I can turn hospital linens
to field grass and wildflowers;
I can bring your body to rest
in any heaven I desire.
I cannot bring you back.

In the alley outside the theatre, I overheard your opinion of the one-man show. That we should put him out to sea on a trash barge. You smoked with authority. Later, you sat at your computer, wrote your column and cut him loose. Each of us, your readers, tied to you like incremental balloons that together gave you flight. I wished that it were me. That I were sitting cross-legged on the mountain of takeout boxes and shit-heavy diapers, wearing the enigmatic smile of fat Buddha. That you would crack the champagne against my bow, bubble over my visible stink, and then wave at me from the shore.

A Love Story

You need to do the laundry. Refinance the mortgage. Reset your broken elbow. Bait the bear trap. Braid your beard. Shave your toes. Set fire to the houseplants. Toss the stroller over a guardrail. Brew a pot of nightshade. Trim back the brambles. Lay out the guest towels. Pin sheets over the doors. Sew new curtains. Cobble new shoes. Donate your hair, clothes, blood, organs, plasma, semen; nobody will take the mattress. Run for Hope. Walk for AIDS. Crawl for Milk. Buy ethical, single-origin cigarettes. Hijack the banana truck. Tighten up. Sweeten down. Arrange tampons in a decorative basket. Make your hands smell like roasted potatoes. Destroy worlds underfoot. The tap is dripping, eating through the washer and valve.

for teaching everything how to talk.

I started with the bird.
That was easy. There were books on the subject.

The dog was a joke. We both liked
to speak for him. It seemed only natural
that he should start conversing with the bird
while we were away.

Then the utensils,
bonded as they were
with our hands and our mouths.
Being simple in purpose and thought,
they were no threat to the order of things.
The spoon's existential drift—
why not me for meat, why always soup
and so forth—
was easy to ignore.

The couch was the first mistake.
Sat-upon, powerfully large, immobile,
it moaned through the night,
trapped inside itself. How long
has it had one broken leg?
Did we really never notice?
Did we decide it didn't matter?

Now everything natters on.
The cliquey dining chairs
gossip in their twos and fours.
The houseplants grumble
as they crane toward the sun,
sulk shut in the evening.
The windows express distaste
for greasy fingerprint smudges.
We'd always assumed
they were happy to be shit on by seagulls.
The desk papers petition for sorting.
I cried, *This house is not a democracy!*

Forgive me. Nothing stops
once given a voice. Not even
by execution. I snapped all the pencils—
that's why there's nothing to write with—
but the pens taught the paper,
the paper taught the bindings.
There is no going back.

I.

I stay up late
because the act of brushing my teeth
and laying my glasses on the bedside table
means admitting there is nothing left to see.

Another day spent feeling tired and stupid
lying on my back in the grass
closing my eyes as patterns of triangles
dance over the lids in muted colours.
Sitting up to look over at a friend
half-asleep in some other private low.
The nearby drummers
beating to the distant sound of our indifference.
This drug like a bad vacation:
the disappointing food, a thing to be endured.

II.

He puts brown sugar
and fresh cracked pepper on the bacon
while his wife puts crème fraiche
and chives from the windowsill in the eggs.
I'm passed out in their living room.
They bring me breakfast
and I tell them their bacon and eggs
taste like no other bacon and eggs I've had.
They smile like one person,
tease, pretend to argue
about who will sleep farthest from the wall
to hold the cats at bay
(*Enough like children,* he says.
For now, she adds
and they laugh).

I rarely see them kiss—
mostly they look at each other.
They both have short blond hair.
My long black thread
on the shower wall
doesn't worry her. She doesn't worry.

FOR RENT

Windows rattle with train cars, one-room
over failing grocery store. Sad-eyed Korean couple
stands behind counter watching vegetables rot.

Former tenant collected antique guns,
could not pay the rent. Loved his grandfather,
sought him in old and broken barrels.

Cat meowed neurotic and shaken at all hours,
never slept, eventually died. Body left behind,
delicate bird skeletons caught in drapes.

Photos of grandfather on bedside, windowsill,
in sink, under bed. No telephone line,
sun appears at eleven and disappears at one.

Cotton sheets threadbare as silk and gravel,
working television in corner. Glows blue,
nightlight eerie, hums lullabies of talk.

Former tenant found on tracks, broken,
did not sully guns with bullets. Wanted:
someone who can pay rent, smoking/pets OK.

FLOORBOARD

I found a crack
where I can yank
and the floorboard comes clean away.
And a loose brick in the foundation
that would take down the house.
And the frequency
at which to sing
to make the earth split apart.
I keep this knowledge

on typewritten cards
bound and tucked inside
the loose skin over my wrist and forearm,
the magician's sleeve I cannot strip—
I keep this knowledge

like a pistol in a pillowcase.
Nudging my head against the safety
as I roll and dream.

And when I take a lover
and press the barrel against their teeth
as they roll and dream,

they never flinch.
Some open their mouths wide, wider.

NO-FAULT DIVORCE / WINTER

Gave a stranger fifty-five cents to ride the last bus
rumbling slowly along the unplowed streets.
He saluted me through the window. I pressed on,

past cars abandoned sideways at the bottom of a hill.
Decorative hedges shorn, branched as coral made of ice.
Street signs pressed in crystal. The city looked wild,

snow stacked haphazardly in the middle of the road,
lost hats and gloves, futile tire tracks. Somewhere,
blankets contoured to bodies, a glimpse of flesh:

glancing light off smothered patio furniture,
indistinct shapes to be dug out or forgotten.
Twenty blocks from home, sky relit by reflection,

I passed under dammed gutters, stalactites glistening.
Home: newly empty bed and sulphurous gas heat,
creak of water pipes almost audible. Cyclical,

inevitable, still no one was prepared. In the wind,
a poignant sting. Such pleasure in our defeat.

You may divide the raisin toast
along the cinnamon line.

The coffee, cleave
into two great black waves.
Leave a path wide enough for Moses and
all the children of Israel.

The sausages, bisect into butterflies,
pin each wing and label the inner anatomy.

Smash the plates over your knee.
Neatly, now: no scattered, minor shards
to be swept out from under the refrigerator.
No bloodied fingers, diamond studs.
No male and female juts
evocative of glue. A perfect break, each plate
the guarded face of the moon, half in shadow.

Ten days of sunshine before ten months of rain.
Fog burns away. The ghostly image of mountains,
spirit kingdoms, craggy as broken glass.

You left Buenos Aires for New York, New York for Bombay,
Bombay for Paris. I'm trying to find beauty
in the overturned bowl of bread dough,
some word for grass other than "green."
I took your skeleton from my closet
and ground your bones for flour.

An electrical fire in Paris: rats chewing on wires,
artists with clamps, cigarettes, strung lights.
Malarial fever in Bombay. She will come to you,
seize you with heat, fry you in your sleep.

I told a sailor I thought owning a boat was pointless.
It just sits in the water and rots. Like a house isn't bad enough.

Moss grows between the folds of my skin.
Scrape and re-varnish. Prop up, hammer grommets.

Frozen eyelashes crunch. The sound
of dead fluttering kiss, ice-crusted wings
scraping a cheek.

Third bus goes by, full.
Impassive faces line the stop,
too polite to huddle for warmth.
A baby in a stroller screams
from its hidden mouth, screams
through layers of plastic down,
a mouthful of saliva and wool.
Why are we out here, he screams,
why is this new world so painful
and dull.

A postcard from Argentina, your
writing loose with Mendoza vino:
the suggestion of a woman,
mentions of heat. You slip
into *La Garganta del Diablo*,
The Throat of the Devil,
as it lies open, tilted backward
over the edge of the bed.
Garganta, the largest waterfall in the world
named for this hell-hot split tongue, this bend,
this right angle of deepest penetration.

You must have been miserable
sometime. This is the only way
I can accept things as they are.

TREE EXPOSED BY LIGHTNING

The tree lies on the crushed house
looking startled, a man who wakes up
in a heap of alley trashbags, kidneys gone.
His rounded back is the still image
of a Tesla ball, a violet tattoo of branches.
The fastest path to the ground passes shoulders
and coils to the spine.

Look at the pulp heroine with her clothes ripped open,
backgammon points of breast,
insides of a tree: under black cinder,
raw sienna, a jagged reveal.
Was there a sound? A whipcrack,
less certain than thunder,
mild vertigo of expecting an extra step.
Then the creak, a warning to the house:
sorry, old friend.

Why do you know where you were
when so-and-so was shot,
when so-and-so pushed the button
and the bombs fell,
when the faces went stern on the television?
Why do those get to be the moments?

When the tree came down,
we ran out into the eye.
We ran from our homes,
from the store and the gas station,
the diner and the bank.
We knew each other's names.

SMALL CRIMES
OF A
NORTHERN PEOPLE

we talk about all the poets
who committed suicide.
The comparative merit
of stones in a pocket
over the gas oven.
"She didn't want to leave
her children alone," we say.
"But she did."

We imply
as modern poets,
we are made of sterner,
less sentimental stuff.
We can weather the draft
through a crack in the bricks,
the presence or absence
of children or fame.

When one of us
commits suicide,
we say he was ill,
not a poet.

LET US CHANGE BODIES

as we might change seats.
Everyone move one to the left,

now you are someone else.
Your teeth are misaligned in a different way,
your vision is wrecked or perfected,
you box people and art with new prejudice.

Your mouth is still mindlessly full: a street pakora,
or clear noodles made of bean curd,
or goat meat shredded and tamped down, or raw liver,
or an electric toothbrush, a lover's finger, a deep-fried scorpion,
all and any of these things suddenly routine.

Now you're someone else,
the sun is crushing your eyelids shut,
sending you fleeing from noon, thirsty
down to the palms of your hands and the soles of your feet.
Now you're someone else,
and the air is tepid bathwater, the grey inoffensive,
leaving you docile and confused about the time of day.

Now you are watching a window
as a wasp trembles in
and ricochets off the kitchen chair like a drunk.
Now you are in a bed that bows as deeply
as a suspension bridge,
cradling a man's head to your chest as he weeps
and you feel your resolve drain away.

Now you are climbing the outer cliffs of a mountain
on a spiritual pilgrimage,
the marker at the top an upstretched hand.
Now you are climbing a mountain
because the landscape forms the profile of a witch
and you were drunk and wanted to prove a local legend wrong.

Now someone is taking your picture,
and you've forgotten how your mouth works;
you mash your lips together with one canine exposed
thinking it's a closed-mouth smile.
Now your grown child is begging you to eat,
but grief has severed the ties between your hand and the spoon.

Now you are paralyzed by your own importance.
Now you are counting fireflies, or stars,
or lit-up homes in a valley.
Pinpoints lives that blink on and then off
or blaze like meteors in the Pleiades,
eclipse the night.

FOUR TEENAGE GIRLS AT
A VIETNAMESE RESTAURANT

are those Nike no Lululemon
they have this v that makes your butt look awesome
and they would hide a thong
did you say you can see my thong
no I said they would hide a thong

remember Ben who I had a crush on
I want to stop taking birth control
I always forget
use something else
wear the patch
over your eye like a pirate
arr mateys I see no babies here
you're so funny

your lip looks puffy
yeah it does did you bite it
no I just have a weirdly thin upper lip
I have a weirdly thin lower lip
yeah you do
I think it's your teeth

she eats a ton of them
but she takes them out of the fridge one at a time
I try not to snack

I hate how you're always on your phone
when I think you're listening to me
or like suddenly watching *Friends*
I think we're having a conversation
and then I hear this noise

I'm obsessed with these new videos
they're not new
they're new-*er*
no those have been around forever

DISSECTION

Cut into a lobster, a crow, a mouse,
an ape, your mother.
See the economy of space inside the body:
a shared rented room in the city.
Fat crowds against the walls,
shoots heroin into his blubbery sac.
Coils of intestine unwind on the futon,
motel maids squeezing shit through
caterpillar rooms of clogged drains,
ruined sheets thin as tissue paper.
Organs sleep tangled in hammocks
like treefuls of mutant, bulbous fruit.
They wake up late for sweatshop jobs
with hair in their mouths.
This is all we are. The grade school maps
have neat highways, systems separate,
one machine function and then the next.
How shocking to see skin split
like dandelions through concrete,
to see how everything is jammed
together with no air between,
no hollows and tubes just
meat and compression like a sink
against a bed against a door.

Jesus steps into the ring,
iconic hands out. Shining white shorts.
The ref takes issue with the crown of thorns.
He slips it off, open sores
where each needle fit, forehead like
a palette of watercolours, all of them red.

At twenty-one,
The Boxer is an old boxer,
a learned-to-lace-his-gloves-in-the-garage kid
who lost baby teeth to left hooks
and natural causes,
second set growing over the first like a shark.
He has dozens of blood brothers.
He is a shadow-chaser, a slow motion fall.
He knows the bones of his inner ear
like most people know their own face.

In this corner, The King of Kings!
Jesus does not pander to the crowd.
The roar gives them a moment to speak.
The Boxer shows the darkness of his throat
in the gaps of his smile, and says,
Lord, I knew you would be good at this.
Clearly it is the sport of gods.

You confuse me with my father,
the Lamb replies.

Ding-ding.

HOW TO SPEAK IN THIS FAMILY

His father begins a joke
and punchlines rush in from all sides:
two men at the pearly gates
oh I know this one a refrigerator fell on
no one of them is Polish and the other is
not a man a blonde girl in a sack of
nun and an army man with a nasty
why aren't you laughing?

His mother says, *Open wide!*
pours hot sauce into the gap
then shakes him by the throat,
squeezing just under the nodes.

His grandmother pushes hot dogs,
fish bones, peach pits
past his tonsils with a stick.

His sister duct-tapes his mouth while he sleeps.
Talk, she demands. *You defective bird.*
Threaded glue around his beak.
Polly wants...!

Eventually the suturing needle comes out
plaster hardens over cotton over lips
then under-nose and chin skin stretched,
shut in a series of nicks and thread:
a laced-up skate.

Listen to the outside.
Cicadas and grasshoppers converse in hushed tones,
pausing between the crest and the trough of the tide.

Talk!

That he was with a friend,
and she was alone. That he
addressed her in English:
Don't, though his accent
was francophone. Not even
the language-neutral
Attention, or the
French-appropriated
cri de coeur
Stop! No, just
Don't. Lazy auxiliary
negation, no verb
to aid. Meaning
he did not think
she was deaf,
staring with such focus
at an aggressive orange hand
blossoming into a whole,
brighter, whiter man.
Meaning he thought
she was just inconsiderate
because her foot dripped
down off the curb
as a siren
screamed from the left.
Meaning someone
as thoughtless
and reckless as she
cannot speak
his language.

Cannot even speak
ambulance.

SMALL ROOMS IN THE LAND OF THE DEAD

A teacher said I would be punished
for my mediocrity
with a tiny apartment
in the land of the dead.
Do the dead still dream of opulence,
far-flung corners, kingdom and carriage?
Or did he mean
ecstatic ghosts would flit by
my mid-level windows,
freed from bondage, angles
of floor to wall and bone to bone?

You will die as you have lived, he said.
The dead sit on a redwood porch
enclosed by fragrant trees
in the icy damp before dawn; the dead
sip hot mugs of coffee,
well-rested from sleep,
contemplate the skitter of a deer
and the slanting hillside.
The dead eat the soft flesh
of ripe peaches
and animals who knew sun.

You'll be a man among gods, he said,
pan dust for bits of broken glass,
suck at raincoats for water,
cradle your broken feet.

The dead rise
to the sounds of their dying,
to the bleat and the screech
and the long pausing breath
and the pleading.
The dead lie stretched out
yellow with gathered blue,
plugged shut with cotton,
penny-eyed or in luminous flame.

The cat is dead. Your cat is dead.
Keeping the bay window open,
letting the snow blow in and bury the furniture,
this post-apocalyptic nuclear winter scene—
it will not bring him back.
You cannot keep the electric heater on full blast,
melting a protective circle around itself,
a lake encroached on all sides by icebergs.
It looks like the last man alive
in a defeated army, blowing out the final magazine
of a machine gun, feet off the ground from the blowback,
the noise futile and powerless as weeping—
and you're going to get electrocuted.
Your cat was hit by a car. Or it died from exposure.
Or that hideous shrieking that sent you
out onto the sidewalk calling his name
was another cat tearing your cat to shreds.
Under a porch somewhere, your cat ignored
the hobo markings on the post, the powerful
three-pronged swipe, the wood whittled down fine,
and feral strays saw your baby for what it was.
Or maybe that was just the hot water in the pipes,
whistling as it stretched the iron, and the neighbours
saw your bare butt for nothing.
There are bus station birds in the rafters,
raccoons in his feeding dish, eating down to where
the wet food started to mould.
The occasional black bear lumbers in from the hill,
noses in the kitchen trash, bats at the scratching post,
stares at you frank and unafraid: the house is theirs now.

Your cat never spoke. Your cat never gave.
Your cat was a projection of your soul
and your soul lives on. Buy a new cat.
Give it the same name.

WHY THIS PLACE AND NOT ANOTHER

A YEAR IN CHARLOTTESVILLE

I.

An epileptic cockroach seizes into the light
from a drawer yanked free.
Exhausted space,
hiding from the heat in the dark.

Intimate space: kitchen through a bedroom
bathroom through a bedroom
front door through a bedroom
the grunt of his coming all around.

Listening to another couple making love
I am surprised by its brevity:
a breath just long enough to begin and end.

Back home,
to resist the compression of your curls,
time rises, spreads its arms, arches its back, lengthens its spine
and expands

A drop of sweat slips from your brow;
gravity watches languidly
remembering to pull at the last moment.

I have been away from you for a day, or a few months,
time small enough to be caught with a single snap of the jaws
tail hanging out in mocking.

II.

Bodies find home in beds.
Bodies can only sojourn on couches
overstay welcomes, drift.

Wake to a still-burning hash pipe,
a stranger's smouldering sleeping breath
entering my mouth,
an armrest fitted into the arch of my back.
Wake to an unconscious crowd
dressed only in paint.

There are more people on the couches now
than when I fell asleep.

I am the only one awakened by birds
pollen and white petals blown in,
the Virginia hot summer hail.
I am the only one awakened by light
quivering with the drugged threat of day.
I am the only one awakened by the upstairs neighbour,

a Christian soldier, marching as to war.
Combat boots beat a steadfast drum
across the ceiling, down the stairs.
He has been awake for hours.

He associates youth with perky tautness
resents the weights we hang from our chins
to make our faces sag,

from our bellies, from our floppy biceps,
from our feet as we drag them across the floor.

In our trash, he finds slashed canvas
an imprint in orange tempera of buttocks and balls.
The world is slow to recognize our genius.

I left you for this.

III.

I have been away from you for a year
living among artists, watching their casual exchange of bodies
growing sick with talk.

Words hold in the heat, tar over the bulbs in my lungs
visible as white rings
puffed from the rounded mouths of sophisticates.

I left them
sharing a jar of pesto for breakfast
their faces beginning to blur into one another.

I thought I saw you at the market
hands wrist-deep in a display of tomatoes
just to finger their plumpness and smooth skins
but you were somewhere else
mouth already full of juice and yellow seeds.

Winnipeg has the highest density
of mosquitoes per square mile
on earth.

Sounds about right, he says.
He remembers the crunch of the windshield wipers.

He remembers running
the two steps from his parents' house to their garage,
seeing them cluster on his bare child legs,
their abdomens stretched into lurid red bulbs,
sapped light and blood.
Together they comprise the devil,
hold his buzzing shape. A holy rejoinder to greed.

What was it like to grow up here? he asks.

Even the sky looks green.
A dome of turquoise glass, oxidized copper,
clouds of mulch.
Nearby, a dog blinks away the rain.

I consider pointing to the spider-bite scar
on my cheek, but it feels like a lie.

Painless, I say.

There is a diner—there are a million—
spooned against the highway, contoured as to a lover's back,
with homemade ice cream and local Americana on the walls:
find all fifty states in the word search on the placemat.
Waitresses in uniform toothy smiles crack bubble gum,
notably young or old, before and after a factory run of babies—
yes, they're real. There is lightning
that is more than a camera flash, an almost-missed trick of the eye.
White snakes that slither and nest, cross distances, grow vast.
They reveal the shape of a pillarless cathedral
with ample time for your slow-motor mind
to recognize *grey* and *purple*: long, long lightning.
      There are hanging lodge lights that flicker with thunder,
windows streaked by rain—not a Hollywood effect,
that rainmaking machine too forceful with its aim too straight,
that trumped-up garden hose—
wooden booths and stove-burnt coffee from
kitchens stalled in the fifties. Cut green beans from a tin,
Fanny's fried chicken. Bugs in crevice refuge—
sky declares war on earth!—or else drown
in puddles with the force of oceans,
their world bombed desolate. Spiders survive on the eaves,
swing wild in sideways torrent.

      A motorcycle hydroplanes slowly past the window
with its wheels locked, as though on a moving walkway,
—a mundane ride through the airport, a trick,
raise the TV camera above their feet and the dancers float.
There are men eating mash and talking of women
in what is thought to be old-fashioned ways—

though crudeness is the first language,
propriety learned and unlearned along the way—
in *yeps* and *nopes* and seldom more. *Waiting out the storm,*
waiting in diners, no question that the storm will end.

I.

A woman in a spotlight with a guitar. I paid money to see her, her distracted happiness. My nervous, despairing heart: we were like longtime lovers at the breakfast table, and she'd met someone else and hadn't told me yet. A breakfast that I'd made, overmade, with absurd flourishes and pretty plating. The other man with egg yolks for eyes, a lewd grin of bacon. She strummed lazily in the spot, spoke in a muted voice like her throat was lined with wool: "I just came back from New York, and…" She shook her head, like that would be enough, we'd understand. "I met someone else, and…" But I pushed, wanting to whittle down the blade, sharpen that first, blunt blow: "Did you fuck him?" Strumming, then: "I fell in love. I can't wait to go back. I'm going to move there." *Twa-YANG-twang*, then: "I think you haven't lived until you've lived in New York." This said to us! Her paying, non-New York audience. We nodded. Yes, we are not living, we have not lived. We are halted wind-up toys, springing into motion each time you come home for Thanksgiving or Christmas or a funeral.

II.

You must know New York City to understand Western literature, as you must know the bible. Its geography, boroughs, parables. You will not need directions. You will not get lost. You have been studying it accidentally your whole life: here is where Elizabeth Smart sat down and wept, here where Dylan Thomas drank himself to death, here where Meg Ryan and Tom Hanks met and met again. Even Brooklyn and Lower Manhattan, where the numbers stop and the streets curl like petals of diseased flowers, even the Rockaways, distant Queens: you have heard it all in a song. Walking up Broadway as though into the sun. The first time you saw *Casablanca*, you knew every line. You dreamt of French-controlled Morocco without knowing, your fingers drawn to the right piano keys.

III.

A recorded voice drones over the film: first the Jews, then the Italians, then the Puerto Ricans, then the Dominicans and the Chinese. Now the hip young whites, the girl beside me on the platform in her tights and glasses, a sense of theft. What seduced you? I asked, as she tucked her wallet deeper into her coat. I told her: I live on almost nothing by the sea, in a hammock tied to the overhang of a fisherman's roof, his children tossing fish guts in the sand. And you, she said, you don't think that you're a thief? At least I stole my whiteness, I replied. Nobody gave it to me.

IV.

We roll through Madison Square Park, lit for Christmas, and I start in
on my spiel: the sea, the fisherman's children, et al. She laughs, chas-
tises me for sins I have not confessed to anyone. She like the new
wife of an ex-lover, insistent on having me over for dinner when I can
think of nothing worse. The meal is infinite, shifting; when I reach
one end of the table, she's begun changing the dishes at the other. She
braids my arms and legs with the arms and legs of strangers, binds
them tight, and we yammer at each other, scamming, conniving, fall-
ing into furious lust. I tell her about the stars I can see at home, the
terror of that pure black in the valley, the directionless web of light
like a child's painted ceiling; she makes her own stars, never sleeps.
We come across a brasserie at three in the morning, drink French 75s,
then back down the block for dollar coffee and Israeli breakfast. She
has no patience for my jokes, my loping gait, my drawl—speak faster,
she says, and funnier and smarter. She feels for the weak spot at the
base of my gut, where I keep all the things I cannot do, the languages
I don't speak, and presses until I start to sing. She asks, snarling, Can
you hear yourself?

PARIS AT DUSK

Sunsets gather in a room
the size of an elevator,
waiting for their audition.
They parade past, one by one,
wearing red zebra-print dresses,
hats with iridescent feathers,
pink leg warmers that bunch
unflatteringly around the calf.
They sing in high, warbling voices,
overact, all daggers and tears,
do that same vanishing act,
hoping the director hasn't been dulled
to just another pretty face.

       You bit a crepe hot from my hand
       on a sidewalk narrow as a bicycle.
       We fell into patio chairs
       that belonged to no one,
       held hands. On the wind,
       veal bones stewed to melt, cigars,
       butter like solace. The smooth oval
       of the fountain pool rippled in dialogue
       with our faces, then spread over the city,
       painting all the buildings
       the colour of a bruised plum.

Our sunset stood on stage
and made predictable choices:
monologue from Shakespeare,
lovers by a fountain in Paris.

Songbirds burst from her mouth,
cleaved the spotlight into *long purples,*
her clothes spread wide.
Then we remembered
why the bard is The Bard,
why we weep for Ophelia,
why the heart still shocks at the sky.

I KNOW WHAT IT WOULD BE LIKE

For andrea bennett

to grow old with you.

I can picture the animals we'd rear
somewhere cold and remote,
the sheltie and the goats.
Companionable silence over boiled coffee,
wraparound flannels. Our shared office
where we work back to back,
watch the goats from the bay window,
knead the sheltie with our feet.

I can picture the simple meals,
the checked plastic tablecloth, going to sleep
at an early dusk. Patting you affectionately
on the shoulder or the knee,
through layers of blanket
across twin beds pushed together.
Beds that shift apart in the night
and leave an impassable gap.

I don't know what it's like to be your lover,
to be young with you,
to despair at the unknowability of your body
and its separation from mine.

I have slept by your side for many nights
and never considered your smell.
I've never been repulsed and fascinated by you,
never considered swallowing you whole.

I don't want to know.

I wouldn't trade the consummation of work
for sex. There are others for that.
I married one, and so did you,
vowed life, sickness, health. But life is short.
The word is infinite. We are bound beyond time.

JULY

I was sick today.
You know
the kind of sickness
I mean.

Tonight,
after the sun goes down—
if it ever goes down—
I will go for a walk.

The night is only
five or six hours long.
Enough time to
get outside the city.
To visit
the Jesus billboards
and their promises
of eternal life.
Step over
the desiccated mouse.
The crow, its barrel chest
bloated with maggots,
dressed in glossy, funereal blacks
and a dignified stare.
Reach the thicket of brambles
where the road ends. I can choose
not to follow the highway,
the railway,
the waterways

into the sticky embrace
of another golden dawn.

I will be sick again
tomorrow. I can feel it
coming on.

We sat on the roof and watched the tornado come,
its morbid beauty growing by the mile. Mother downstairs
in a morphine coma, no longer wailing, "comfortable."
Wooden sidewalks of neighbouring shackle towns
had their boards ripped out, spun wet then dry.
I'd arrived with tarp and hammer and nails,
ready to batten down. "Too late," the doctors said.
Already people were standing on their porches,
holding hands, accepting the jaundiced sky:
Mother's eyes shut, sealed. Even the priest
stood silently, not suggesting we pray or repent,
no manic tarantella of I-told-you-so. A quiet apocalypse.
Children and dogs in their near heaven knowing,
trees bending acquiescent as reeds.
Mother sings names in her sleep, wheezing:
insistent wind through cracks in the windows.
My sister asks if anyone wants tea. The kettle blows.
This is how death comes, in the modern miracle,
gentle rain and a long, distant whistle.

ACKNOWLEDGEMENTS

Thanks to:

My writing-soulmate, andrea bennett.

My soulmate-soulmate, John-Paul Lobos.

Keith Maillard and the poets of the UBC MFA program from 2009–11, a band of geniuses and lunatics that included Ben Rawluk, Emily Davidson, Kevin Spenst, Melissa Sawatsky, Karen Shklanka, Margret Bollerup, Rhea Tregebov, Anna Maxymiu, Michelle Deines, Elizabeth Ross and Ray Hsu.

Esther McPhee, Kaitlin Fontana, Erika Thorkelson, Bill Radford, Rebecca Brown, Tim Mak and Jacob Sheehy; they know what they did.

My editor at Nightwood, Silas White, who wrangled this book into shape, and everyone else at Nightwood, who helped usher it into the world.

The Canada Council for the Arts.

The magazine editors who provided beacons of hope along the way, at *Room*, *The New Quarterly*, *Grain*, *Carousel*, *PRISM International*, *Ricepaper*, *Poetry Is Dead*, *Numero Cinq* and *The Rusty Toque*.

My family, the Fus, Loys, Loboses, Negilskis and Dutrizacs. But especially the Fus, who have had to put up with me the longest.

ABOUT THE AUTHOR

Kim Fu's debut novel *For Today I Am a Boy* (2014) was a finalist for the PEN/Hemingway Award, a *New York Times Book Review* Editor's Choice, winner of the Edmund White Award and long-listed for Canada Reads, among other honours. Fu's writing has been widely published and anthologized, including by *The Atlantic, NPR, Maisonneuve* and *Best Canadian Essays.* Fu is a graduate of the University of British Columbia with an MFA in Creative Writing. She was a 2015 Writer-in-Residence at Berton House in Dawson City, Yukon, and a 2016 Ucross Foundation Fellow. She lives in Seattle, Washington.

PHOTO CREDIT: LAURA D'ALESSANDRO